CRABTREE CONTACT

HI TECH WORLD: CODE BREAKERS

Ben Hubbard

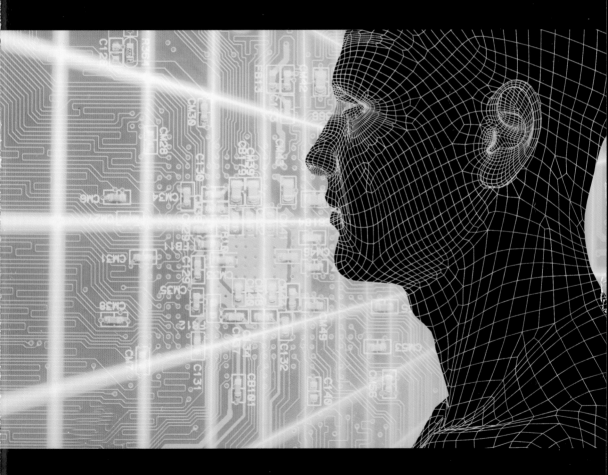

🌱 Crabtree Publishing Company

www.crabtreebooks.com

Crabtree Publishing Company

www.crabtreebooks.com   1-800-387-7650

PMB 59051   616 Welland Avenue,
350 Fifth Avenue, 59th Floor   St. Catharines, Ontario
New York, NY, 10118   L2M 5V6

Content development by   Published by
Shakespeare Squared   Crabtree Publishing
                               Company © 2010
www.ShakespeareSquared.com
                               First published
in Great Britain in
2010 by TickTock
Entertainment Ltd.

Printed in the
U.S.A./122009
CG20091120

Crabtree Publishing
Company credits:
Project manager: Kathy Middleton
Editor: Reagan Miller
Production coordinator: Katherine Berti
Prepress technician: Katherine Berti

TickTock credits:
Publisher: Melissa Fairley
Art director: Faith Booker
Editor: Victoria Garrard
Designer: Emma Randall
Production controller: Ed Green
Production manager: Suzy Kelly

Thank you to Lorraine Petersen and the members of nasen

Picture credits (t=top; b=bottom; c=centre; l=left; r=right; OFC=outside front cover;
OBC=outside back cover): A. Barrington Brown/Science Photo Library: 7tr.
AFP/Getty Images: 24. Bettmann/Corbis: 14, 15. iStock: OFCl, OFCr, 1, 25, 27.
Mehau Kulyk/Science Photo Library: 28–29. Stephen Mulcahey/Alamy: 12–13.
Science and Society/ SuperStock: 8–9. Science Source/Science Photo Library: 7tl,
7tc. Shutterstock: OFC (background), 2, 4 (both), 5, 6–7, 10, 11 (both), 16t, 20–21,
22, 23, 26, OBC (background). SSPL via Getty Images: 16b, 19. Volker Steger/
Science Photo Library: 29. Time & Life Pictures/Getty Images: 17, 18.

Every effort has been made to trace copyright holders, and we apologize in advance
for any omissions. We would be pleased to insert the appropriate acknowledgments
in any subsequent edition of this publication.

Library and Archives Canada Cataloguing in Publication

Hubbard, Ben
      Hi tech world : code breakers / Ben Hubbard.

(Crabtree contact)
Includes index.
ISBN 978-0-7787-7528-7 (bound).–ISBN 978-0-7787-7550-8 (pbk.)

      1. Cryptography--History--Juvenile literature.
2. Ciphers--History--Juvenile literature. 3. Computer
hackers--Juvenile literature. 4. Data encryption (Computer
science)--Juvenile literature. I. Title. II. Series: Crabtree contact

Z103.3.H82 2010   j652'.8   C2009-906927-X

Library of Congress Cataloging-in-Publication Data

Hubbard, Ben.
  Hi tech world : code breakers / Ben Hubbard.
      p. cm. -- (Crabtree contact)
  Includes index.
  ISBN 978-0-7787-7528-7 (reinforced lib. bdg. : alk. paper) --
ISBN 978-0-7787-7550-8 (pbk. : alk. paper)
  1. Computer security--Juvenile literature. 2. Computer hackers--
Juvenile literature. 3. Data encryption (Computer science)--
Juvenile literature. I. Title.

  QA76.9.A25H846 2010
  005.8--dc22

                                                    2009048028

Computer programing code

CONTENTS

INTRODUCTION

For as long as there has been written information, there have been codes.

Throughout history, codes have kept information secret:

- In ancient times, leaders sent coded orders to their armies.
- Secret government papers were written in code to protect the contents.
- **Spies** sent coded messages about their enemies.

But as long as there have been codes, there have also been people trying to break them.

When computers were invented, machines partly replaced humans as code breakers.

NATURE'S CODE

Most codes have been created by humans or machines. But the most complicated code was created by nature. It is called DNA.

DNA is found in cells. DNA is the **genetic** code of a living thing. Your DNA is responsible for the color of your eyes and how tall you are. Except for identical twins, no two people have the same DNA. It is your DNA that makes you unique!

double helix

Nobody knew much about this genetic code until the 1950s, when scientists Rosalind Franklin, James Watson, and Francis Crick made the breakthrough. They discovered that DNA looked like two spirals, called a double **helix**.

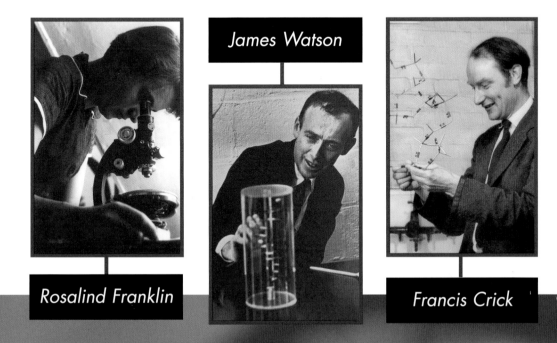

Rosalind Franklin

James Watson

Francis Crick

CODE MAKERS

AND BREAKERS

a re-creation of equipment used by code breakers at Bletchley Park in 1942

A person who turns writing into a secret code is called a cryptographer.

Creating a code is called **encryption**.

A person who breaks a
cryptographer's code
is called a cryptanalyst.

Throughout history, cryptographers
have thought their codes were
unbreakable. But cryptanalysts
have proved them wrong.

THE LOST CODE

We know codes have been around for as long as human history. So what if there were codes that had been lost over time?

Some people believe a forgotten code was used by people across the world thousands of years ago. Some suggest ancient civilizations used this code to build temples, palaces, and tombs in specific locations on different continents.

Stonehenge, England

Some people think the code was part of an early **Global Positioning System** (GPS). They believe the location of Stonehenge somehow links directly to the Great Pyramid in Egypt. They also believe modern GPS is helping to prove the code is real.

Others say such links are **coincidence**, and ancient codes never existed.

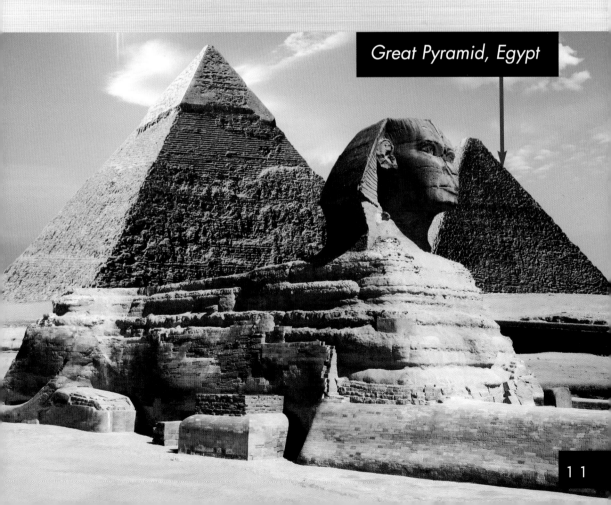

Great Pyramid, Egypt

THE CAESAR SHIFT

The Roman leader Julius Caesar invented a simple letter code.

Caesar wrote a message and then replaced each letter with the letter in the alphabet three places ahead.

For example, "A" would be written as "D" and "B" would be written as "E."

Sometimes the code would change to four or five places ahead in the alphabet in case the first code was broken by enemies.

NAVAJO TALKERS

During World War II, the United States military needed a new code to keep its messages secret from the Japanese army.

Navajo warriors

It was suggested that the Native American nation called the **Navajo** had a code that could help.

This is how the code worked:

In the Navajo language, ba-goshi means "cow." So in a message, ba-goshi would stand for the English letter "C"—the first letter of cow.

Navajo code talker

About 400 Navajo soldiers worked as code talkers. They sent and received messages using their unique code. The Japanese code breakers never broke the code.

ENIGMA

By World War II, the Germans had created the greatest code-making machine ever invented.

The machine was called Enigma and the odds of breaking its code were 150 trillion to one.

In 1939, **mathematician** Marian Rejewski built a model Enigma to try to crack its code. When war broke out, he sent everything he had learned to the code breakers based at Bletchley Park, England.

In 1940, Alan Turing (see pages 18–19), cracked the Enigma's code. From that point on the **Allied** troops could unscramble Germany's many codes.

German soldiers sending a message using the Enigma machine

ALAN TURING

Name: Alan Turing
Profile: English mathematician, code breaker, and one of the founders of modern computer science
Code broken: Enigma
Year: 1940

Alan designed many of the earliest computers used in the U.K., including the Turing machine and the Pilot ACE computer.

Turing also proved that computers are not capable of solving all mathematical problems.

Pilot ACE computer

"We can only see a short distance ahead, but we can see plenty there that needs to be done."
– Alan Turing

COMPUTER CODES

The Enigma machine changed cryptography forever. Now computers could create codes.

The most common modern computer code is called "public key encryption." This code uses a public key and a private key. The public key is used to encrypt text, such as an email. The private key is then used to read this encoded text.

Many people can use the public key to encrypt information. However, only the person with the private key will be able to read the information. This allows people to send private information to each other securely.

COMPUTER HACKERS

Today, computers constantly encrypt information.

This prevents people from stealing our credit card information or reading our emails.

But if there is a code to break, there will always be code breakers hoping to crack it.

The modern cryptanalyst is the computer **hacker**. Hackers illegally break into top secret computer systems.

computer programing code

Some hackers break into computer systems to steal information or to prove computer systems are not secure. **Others just do it for the challenge.**

GARY McKINNON

Name: Gary McKinnon
Profile: suspected computer hacker who has been called "the biggest military computer hacker of all time"
Codes broken: Gary hacked into U.S. government agency computers belonging to the National Aeronautics and Space Administration (NASA), the U.S. Army, Navy, and Air Force, and the Department of Defense.
Year: 2001–2002
Other information: Gary said he was hacking to look for evidence of unidentified flying objects (UFOs).

CAPTCHA

Hackers love to crack computer codes, but can a computer crack a human code?

You have probably seen a CAPTCHA code. It often pops up on a Web site as a line of wavy letters, which you have to type in.

CAPTCHA code

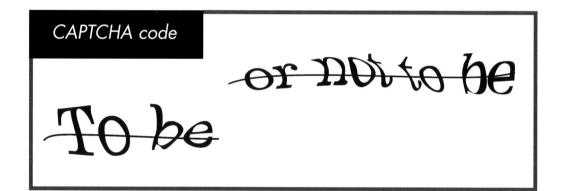

The CAPTCHA code makes sure the user is an actual person. It stops computers from automatically sending spam and viruses to other computers.

But hackers are programing computers to break CAPTCHA codes. Some experts think this will lead to artificial intelligence (AI)—the ability for computers to think for themselves.

QUANTUM COMPUTERS

Making and breaking codes has always relied on mathematics—calculated either by people or computers.

But soon quantum computers will make the codes for us. They are the supercomputers of the future. These computers are based on **physics**, not mathematics.

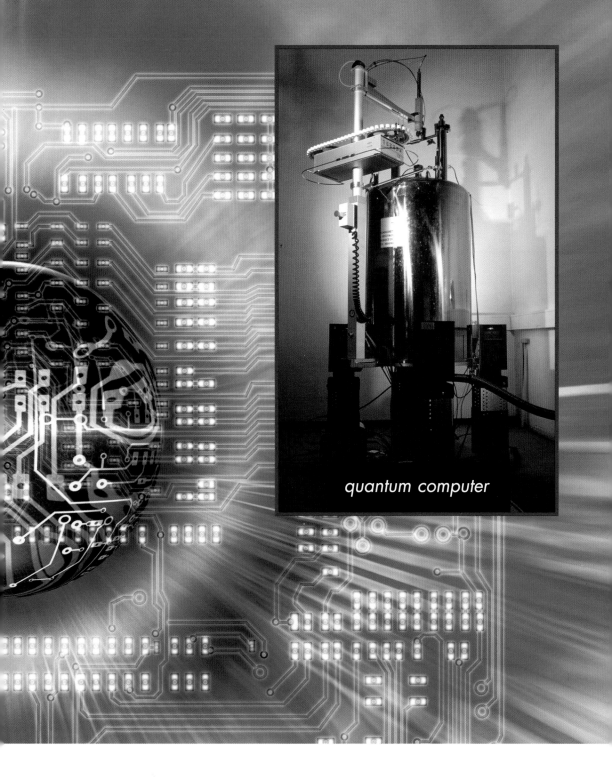

quantum computer

Scientists know that quantum computers will be able to break any code created up to now. They will also be able to make codes that are unbreakable by regular computers.

NEED-TO-KNOW WORDS

Allied United for a cause; often used to refer to the United States, Canada, Great Britain, and other countries who came together to fight Germany and its supporters during World War II

coincidence Things happening at the same time or place by chance

DNA Deoxyribonucleic acid; a type of acid that carries the genetic information in a cell

encrypt To put information into a code so that unauthorized people cannot read it

genetic Related to inherited traits in plants and animals

Global Positioning System (GPS) A navigational system that uses satellites to give exact locations

hacker Someone who uses programing skills to gain illegal access to a computer

helix A spiral shape or structure

hieroglyphs A writing system used in ancient Egypt

mathematician An expert in mathematics

Navajo A Native American nation or group of people

physics A type of science that deals with matter and energy

spy A special agent employed by a person or country to find out secret information

DID YOU KNOW?

- Nobody could read Egyptian **hieroglyphs** until 1799, after the famous Rosetta stone was found. The Rosetta stone is a large stone with a message carved into it in three different languages: hieroglyphic, Demotic, and Greek. Jean-François Champollion was able to translate the hieroglyphs from the writing inscribed on the stone.

FIND OUT MORE ONLINE

Read about a number of different types of codes and try them out for yourself.
www.thedavincigame.com/Code_breaking.html

National Security Agency (NSA) CryptKids Web site, for future code makers and code breakers
www.nsa.gov/kids

Visit this Web site to learn more about sending and receiving messages in code.
www.scienceyear.com/outthere/index.html?page=/ outthere/spy/index.html

INDEX